Outapiaries
And Their Management

M.G. Dadant

Revised by:

Wayne Flewelling, JR.

DEDICATION

This book is dedicated to my Grandpa, Gene Kelly. My grandpa always taught me to chase my dreams and to never give up. He taught me patience when I didn't think I had any. He encouraged me to try again when I failed the first time. He also helped me build my first bee equipment and I still have the nucs he built that I use for my queen mating nucs. But most of all he taught me that no matter what you do, do it with all your heart, and to love with all you have.

CONTENTS

ACKNOWLEDGMENTS

First and foremost I must acknowledge M.G. Dadant for writing this text over 100 years ago. With his dedication to the beekeeping industry as a whole and as the editor of the American Bee Journal, he taught countless beekeepers how to keep and raise healthy bees. His revisions to the Hive and The Honey Bee helped me learn not only the basics but also how to properly care for my bees. And as my apiary grew, this book, helped me expand and grow in a manner that was consistent and practical.

M.G. Dadant

Forward

As I have grown from two hives in my back yard to the large operation I am today spread out over four counties in Kansas, this book was always in my mind of something that I wanted to bring to more people. There is no other book out there that gives practical advice to the small backyard beekeeper on how to grow their operation and establish outapiaries. When I found this script I realized that here was a practical guide that told me how to do it. The advice that was given by Mr M.G Dadant over 100 years ago is still relevant today. Not much has changed in the way we keep bees other than the tracheal mite and the varrora mite. These two small pests have changed the way we keep bees. I don't go into depth on either of these pests in this manuscript as there are many practical books on how to keep your bees healthy. Although times have changed, some methods have changed but basic beekeeping has not changed very much from when this book was first written

M.G. Dadant

PREFACE

Increased demand for honey, better means of transport to outyards, and consequent increased interest in beekeeping as a pursuit have changed many smaller beekeepers into outapiarists. This volume, I hope, may, in some degree, aid the beginning outapiarist in planning and managing their system of apiaries. The marketing of honey, though it is connected closely with the outapiarist, is not treated in this book. It is a subject, however, which has not had its share of attention from the beekeeper. Were better methods of distribution striven for as are methods of production, the demand for our product would be almost unlimited. The writer is specially indebted to his father, brothers, and to Mr. Frank C. Pellett for ideas and information embodied with his own in this book. The cuts have, nearly all of them, appeared in the American Bee Journal for which they were made by Mr. Pellett.

.

CHAPTER I

PREREQUISITES

When the beekeeper outgrows beekeeping in their home apiary and decides to take up outapiary work, it is assumed that this is done with the main object of increasing their income.

It is therefore evident that it is desired to eliminate the non-essentials and to formulate a plan that will give them the greatest returns for the least labor involved. They must make the most out of the apiary always, but they should do it in the least time and not sacrifice themselves to petty details to the detriment of their ever-growing industry. The grass may not be well kept, the hives may be out of level, but the other extreme of minute exactness in outapiary work is nearly as bad as lack of care, at least financially.

Experiments as a rule will, or should be, confined to the home apiary, in which more time may be spent and more careful supervision given, though the keeping of outapiaries will give opportunity for a larger variety of experiments and room for more general observation on many subjects.

In the early days of outapiaries it was considered good practice to keep a person at each apiary during the summer. In some instances now, where very large outapiaries are possible, a helper is kept at each yard during the swarming season. But with the coming of the automobile and truck, and with better roads, it is the usual practice to handle all yards from a central home apiary or from several central apiaries if the system is sufficiently large to warrant division of control.

The Beginnings of Outapiaries

Too many of us are apt to assume that outapiaries are of but recent development, that they have been in operation but a few years. Yet two of America's pioneer beekeepers were able to handle their bees in several apiaries and made a success of producing and selling honey. As early as 1869 John Harbison of California was mentioned as having several hundred colonies scattered in different localities, while Adam Grimm, one of Wisconsin's most noted beekeepers, was considered a prominent authority on hauling bees to outapiaries, the overstocking of localities, etc. Their writings on these subjects appeared in the American Bee Journal as early as 1874.

Today the Adee's of Bruce, SD run in excess of forty thousand colonies in hundreds of outapiaries in North and South Dakota. The advent of large trucks and good roads has enabled todays beekeepers to grow to sizes that could only be imagined in the early days of the first outapiaries.

Dependent on the Person

It will be useless to try to give a definite plan in this book whereby anyone can keep bees either at home or in the outapiary and be uniformly successful. Success will depend chiefly on the person. They must first of all be a successful beekeeper in their home apiary. A beekeeper who cannot make a success of their home yard should not attempt the more difficult outapiary management, for they will surely fail.

Furthermore, they should have their heart in their work. Nor must they be so wrapped in details that they cannot give up some of these in order to make their plans correspond to the demands of their increased holdings.

Prime Requisites

The beekeeper should decide before launching into outapiary work, as to the kind of hive they are to use. It should, as much as possible, be elastic enough to fit in with their system, hearing in mind that non-swarming should be one of the prime requisites; especially is this true with the outapiary, where only occasional visits are made.

Today's choices are of course of the Langstroth design. Either eight frame or ten frame equipment can be used. Eight frame equipment being lighter when full of brood and honey compared to standard ten frame equipment. Another advantage of eight frame equipment some claim is that the outer two frames in ten frame equipment hardly ever get used by the bees anyway and that eight frame equipment more mimics the natural tree cavity.

Then the choice for the modern beekeeper is to run all deeps, 9 5/8 inch boxes or all mediums, 6 5/8", or a combination of the two.

General Subjects Given Limited Treatment

Their bees should be of good energetic stock, disease resistant, and as nearly non-swarming as is possible. Unless they have had experience with other races, they can do no better than to stick to pure Italian stock.

It will be impossible in this book to give detailed plans of operations on specific subjects such as swarm control, disease, wintering, increase, and honey production.

These subjects will necessarily be treated only as they apply specifically to outapiaries, and the reader is advised to make a study of each subject in connection with some good text book on beekeeping. Subjects more generally applicable to outapiaries such as moving of bees, honey houses, automobiles and conveyances, etc. will be more fully treated.

Extracted honey will be discussed mostly since it lends itself best to the outapiary.

Fig. 1. The late John Harbison of California, one of the pioneers in the production of honey in outapiaries.

CHAPTER II

CHOOSING A LOCATION

For many years there has been conducted, in the American Bee Journal, a department to answer questions for beginners and veteran beekeepers alike. Probably one of the questions most frequently asked is "Where shall I locate?"

Desirable Place to Live

This question cannot be answered to the satisfaction of all, since each person has considerations outside of beekeeping which will affect their choice. The climate, a home, educational facilities for their children, etc., will have a bearing on nearly everyone. One person might not like, or their family might not be able to stand, the rigors of a Montana winter, another might balk at the dampness of an Arkansas bottom, while another might prefer the solitude of a California ranch to the busy life nearer the larger cities. Still another might desire the higher altitudes for reasons of health.

Many will have established themselves and will hesitate to leave old associates and ties already made, only in order to increase the honey yield.

Granted, however, that this has been taken into consideration, and that the questioner is concerned only with the value of locating for honey production, there are several things which should be taken into account before final decision is made, and moreover, such final decision should be reserved until personal inspection of the place has been carefully made by the beekeeper. Too many have located only on the advice of some friend or on the suggestion of some article about a certain section, laying stress on the desirable features of such location while omitting the drawbacks, which in themselves might alter the situation.

We have in mind a veterinarian who left a certain section previously recommended to him. It was an excellent place for their practice, but they held fleas in abhorrence, and they abounded there.

Fig. 2. Minor Honey plants are useful in helping stimulate brood rearing.

Honey and Pollen

A first class place for honey production must be one containing honey plants in sufficient quantity to assure at least one main flow during the year. The best places being those which contain the greatest profusion of plants, and are capable of guaranteeing the largest surplus yield.

In the white clover regions, of the East and Central West, those places are most sought after which have another main flow besides the clover, because the clover flow is not certain. A basswood location or sweet clover, buckwheat, or fall flowers combine well with white clover, while a location containing a number of these would be preferable to one with only two flows.

Naturally, we might conceive of a location having all of these flowers which would be only of minor importance in honey production, from the fact that such plants were not in sufficient abundance to make a surplus flow, while another location containing clover alone, might give such enormous crops in good seasons as to overbalance failures of short years.

In the West, alfalfa and sweet clover make a good combination; in the Pacific belt, sage, sweet clover, alfalfa, bean, orange, and other locations are sought.

Climatic conditions are a determining factor in nectar secretion. Some apparently good clover locations are not of the best because climatic conditions are not good during the period of the honey flow, or the summer becomes so dry that the clover "burns out" and a complete failure follows. Average rainfall and average temperature should be carefully studied. Irrigated districts here have an advantage, for the moisture is in stable quantity and removes one uncertainty from the crop.

It is not only the main honey flowers which must be considered however, minor honey plants may help greatly in building up the colonies in the early spring. Pollen plants will induce brood rearing, though it is possible to some extent to supplement early pollen artificially. Minor honey plants may also encourage brood rearing between flows in the summer or fall, when otherwise, the colony would depopulate to such an extent that little of the second or third crop might be secured. Also a small flow in early fall may stimulate brood rearing, thus putting the bees into winter quarters with a large force of young bees. M. V. Facey of Minnesota asserts that the largest variety of honey plants is to be found in a " broken' county. The low lands will furnish late flowers, while the trees and plants of the hills and uplands will, in ordinary seasons, give a continual source of honey from early spring to late fall.

With today's farming practices, honey producers have seen a large decline in honey production. No-till farming uses chemicals to sterilize the land before planting which kills the white clovers, the minor honey plants and other nectar producing plants. This has made it much tougher for the modern beekeeper to produce the kinds of yields that producers of the past have done.

Overstocking

It may be that after such a location has been found, the beekeeper will discover the territory already occupied with bees and in danger of overstocking if another beekeeper with a series of apiaries establishes themselves in this locality.

Although there is no law preventing overstocking or protecting the old established beekeeper in their location against the new, yet it is a pretty well observed unwritten law that an already established beekeeper should be protected in their rights of pasturage in the vicinity surrounding their apiaries. Besides, it would be folly to begin new apiaries under such handicaps, since the per colony production would not only be cut down for the established person, but for the newcomer as well.

The specific question as to what overstocking of a locality is, will be treated in another chapter. It would be our advice to the new beekeeper to consider well before setting in a section already taken up by extensive beekeepers, and probably the best way to get an idea of the possibilities of such locations is by intimate conversation with these beekeepers.

Fig. 3. A broken land furnishes the greatest diversity of flora

No Foulbrood

The up-to-date beekeeper knows how to combat disease, and may, with care and persistent work, rid their apiaries of both European and American foulbrood. But it would be a great relief if it were possible to locate in a section entirely free from disease. Outside of losses caused by applying disease remedies, the labor will be reduced greatly where it is not necessary always to be on the alert for foulbrood.

Many a manipulation practiced in the locality without disease is impossible where foulbrood exists. Beekeepers hesitate to interchange combs, to strengthen weak colonies from the strong, and some, even, do not raise extracted honey because of the fear that foulbrood will necessitate the destruction of many extracting combs. One prominent beekeeper in Illinois has built up a nice bulk-honey business by running entirely for comb honey in shallow frames and buying extracted honey to pack with it.

Naturally, states which have well balanced foulbrood laws and extension departments where beekeeping is in the hands of specialists will be preferred.

Fig. 4. Bees gathered around two buckets of rye chop which had been set out in early spring during a dearth of natural pollen,

Nearness to Market

Depending on whether the beekeeper expects to wholesale their honey in large quantities or whether they wish to work up a retail trade for their own brand, they should decide whether to place themselves near to their markets or can afford to be further away. The working up of a special retail trade in many ways offers advantages. It occupies the time of the producer when work is slackest in the apiary. It gives him a better price for their product.

The item of transportation is not a small one. There are excellent locations for bees which are slow to be taken up because they are a long distance from a railroad and the haul over rough roads is expensive. The advent of the automobile and truck make it possible for outapiary beekeeping and is lessening this objectionable feature, but the transportation expense is still there.

It may pay the beekeeper to live nearer their markets even though they produces much less honey.

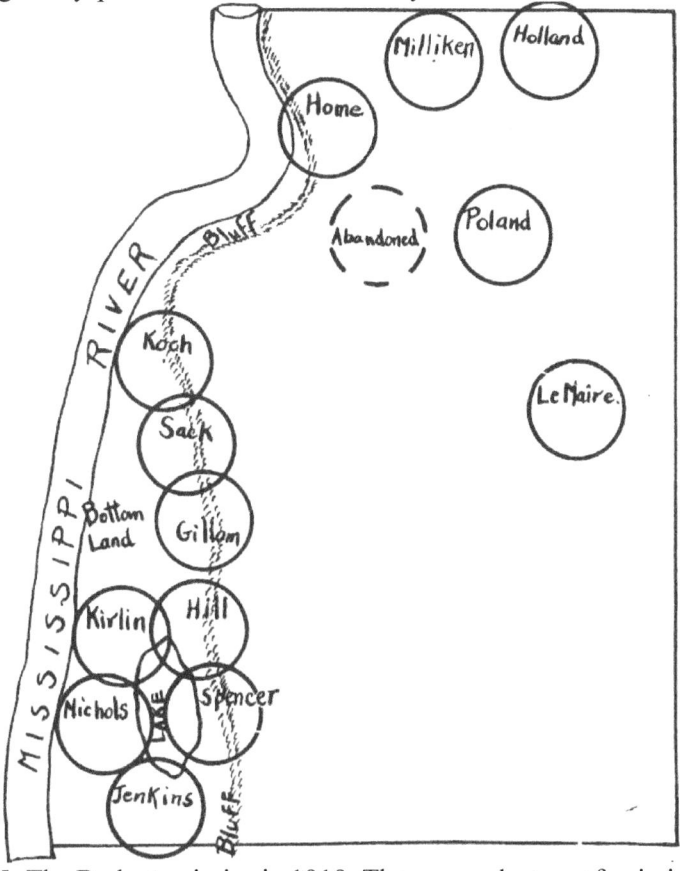

Fig. 5. The Dadant apiaries in 1919. The upper clusters of apiaries are primarily clover locations. Those in the bottom-land are temporary locations to which bees are moved for the fall flow, while the five bluff locations are a combination for both clover and fall flow. It is hard to overstock the bottom locations during a heavy fall flow. The circles represent a diameter of 4 miles, with the apiary in the center.

M.G. Dadant

CHAPTER III

SELECTING APIARY SITES

Having chosen their general location, it remains for the beekeeper to select sites for their individual apiaries. With the object in view of an ever increasing business, these apiaries should be located with due respect to each other and to the home yard, to make the work as systematic as possible. With most outapiarists using automobiles, to do their work, it is oftentimes possible to visit several apiaries in a day, and for this, especially, the apiaries should be arranged in series, having, for instance, three or four apiaries in one general direction so they may be reached on the same trip without too much extra time spent on the road.

Other things being equal, it would be a mistake to locate one apiary ten miles south and the other ten miles north of the home yard when they might be placed in the same general direction and four or five miles apart.

Distance Apart

As a general rule apiaries of any size should not be located less than two miles apart, and if the terrain is not limited, it would be well to increase this distance to four or five miles. It takes little time with a horse, and still less with a car, to travel the extra two or three miles when this would be an advantage rather than have the pasturage overlap.

This matter of distance makes less difference in a bountiful season than in a poor one. In the white clover regions during a heavy flow it is doubtful whether bees go farther than, a mile in search of nectar, and it is certain that the bulk of their harvest is procured much nearer than this. But the beekeeper has not only to consider the heavy flow, but also the light flows and honey dearth. They must arrange their apiaries so that they will be most advantageously located for the bad season as well as the good.

The shape of the country sometimes has a great deal to do with the distance bees will fly to get nectar. Instances have been noted where bees went as far as six miles for nectar. Over hills and woods bees will fly less distance than over a level prairie or down an unbroken valley.

Honey Flora

Not only in choosing their general location, but in choosing each apiary site, the beekeeper must be guided largely by the flora afforded. There is a wide range of flora sometimes in a restricted territory, and it may be possible to increase the yield to an appreciable extent by observing the rules which apply in deciding upon the general apiary site the one which has the greatest variety of honey and pollen flowers, besides having the best opportunity for major honey flows from the more important plants.

A shift of location of a mile or two, especially in a broken country, may give your bees access to a honey flow which they might otherwise miss. It may even be advisable to change the location for a single season to place the apiary near a large field of alsike, sweet clover, buckwheat, or similar plant.

Good note taking of each years yield will give the beekeeper an indication on how each location is producing so that over several years a consensus can be had to keep or move locations.

Good Roads

The location, if possible, should be on good roads, which will allow of trips and examinations even in most unfavorable weather. Spring trips, for feeding and early examinations, often have to be taken at a time when roads are at their worst, and it is something in its favor if the apiary can be reached without undue effort.

Then, too, there is the hauling away of the surplus crop, the re-queening, and other examinations, which must be done at the stipulated time, muddy roads or not.

Fig. 6. The apiary should be located well above the flood mark of highest water.

High Ground, etc.

It is not advisable to locate in a marshy basin where there is recurrent danger of standing water and even floods. The apiary should be on fairly high ground, and in all cases, the hives should be placed so they may not stand in the water, or if it is necessary to use such a location, hives should be protected, as they are in sections of Florida, by being raised on scaffolds high enough to be beyond the danger of rising and receding waters. In these instances the roads are water and trips are made by skiff or motor boat. The late O.O. Poppleton, long idea hive advocate, was very successful with their Florida apiaries, all of which were located so as to be approached by motor boat.

Windbreaks

Especially in northern latitudes where wintering is one of the main problems, it is desirable to so locate the apiary that it will be protected from the prevailing winds. This may be done in one of several ways. Coggshall of New York, advised placing the apiary near a wood so that the force of the wind would be broken, or within a double row of shrubbery or evergreens.

Fig. 7. A slope furnishes the most natural windbreak. Dadant home apiary where bees have been kept continuously for over forty years.

Another good way is to locate on a slope, away from the prevailing winds, which would be usually, in the northern hemisphere, on a southern or south-eastern slope. This would have the added advantage of giving the bees the sun's rays to keep them warm, though in rare instances there might be danger of the bees being enticed to fly when the air was yet too cool, resulting in a loss of chilled bees outside the hive.

Artificial windbreaks are frequently used. High fences are often placed on the north and west of apiaries to turn the wind, while some beekeepers believe that a slatted fence is better. The slatted fence, they argue, breaks the force of the wind while a tight fence deflects the wind upwards, creating a vacuum and causing an undercurrent which is as bad as the wind itself. Then too, the tight board fence is apt to cause snow drifts covering the first row of hives if they are placed close to the fence.

Fig. 8. Some beekeepers use a slatted fence as windbreak. This fence breaks the force of the wind but does not cause drifting of snow. A Fettit apiary in Ontario.

Shade

In warmer climates, shade for the hives is desirable, although there is but little doubt that broken shade is preferable to a dense shade during the whole of the day. Too much shade is apt to delay the bees in getting out in the morning and it also holds the bees in the hive earlier in the evening. Too dense shade in hot weather causes lack of air circulation. Colonies may suffocate and combs melt down under the most unfavorable conditions.

In small hive beetle areas it is not advisable to have hives in too much shade. This not only enables the beetles to breed but can also encourage the formation of chalkbrood. A sunny location will help keep both at bay.

Fig. 9. A brush fence at the back of one of the Rauchfuss apiaries in Colorado, that serves the double purpose of breaking the force of the wind in winter and raising the line of flight of bees in summer, so that they do not disturb passers-by.

Some adjust the matter by using shade boards over the cover of the hive. There is little doubt however, that a reasonable amount of natural shade is beneficial, and to the beekeeper at work as well as to the bees.

In New Mexico, Arizona, and parts of California, on the plains where natural shade is lacking, the apiarist builds a "ramada" or sort of shed covered with long grass, under which the bees are placed in double rows, back to back, with an alley way between. In such locations shade is well-nigh indispensable,

Fig. 10. A Kansas apiary protected by a natural windbreak.

Fig. 11. "Ramada" in New Mexico which serves as a shade for the beekeeper while they work as well as for the bees.

Other Considerations

If the apiary is to be placed with other people and partly in their care, the beekeeper must exercise judgment in choice of families. A person who lets their cows run upon the roads, leaves their fences out of repair, and has things at loose ends about the premises is hardly the person with whom to place your bees.

When possible it is advisable to place the apiary within sight of a house to reduce the danger of depredations to a minimum, and it should be near enough to the main traveled road, but remembering that angry bees are apt to travel twenty rods or more to seek revenge.

In case it is intended to use a building already on the premises as a honey-house, the apiary should be as readily accessible as possible to the honey-house.

CHAPTER IV

BASIS OF PLACING THE APIARY

Probably the two best ways to locate apiaries would be either to own the ground upon which you expect to place your bees or have some relative own it. It may be possible, in many instances to purchase an acre or two in the desired location or to lease it for a long term of years.

However, not being able to purchase the desired spot, and having no relative fortunately located directly in the path of your proposed apiary, the only thing remaining is to make arrangements with the existing forces, namely, the occupants of the location chosen.

Owner Not Renter

Where possible choose a land owner and not a renter, and one who seems to be satisfied with their location with no desire to change. It is annoying, after having gone to some lengths to choose and arrange your location, to be moved off by the next renter who does not like bees, or the next purchaser of the farm who does not care to be "bothered" with them.

Where the location is sought for only a single season such considerations are not of so much weight, but we presume that a majority of locations are desired permanently, and it is in these instances that it is wise to choose well the person and family with whom you try to make arrangements for your apiary.

Rental Price

There are three possible ways of arranging for rental in placing bees; by share, cash, or gift. It is only occasionally that the land owner is willing to allow the bees on their place without compensation; and why should the beekeeper ask it? No doubt that in many instances the bees do the farmer much good through increased fertility of plants, but the beekeeper is getting value received and should pay for it.

In times past, more than now, a share rental varying from a fifth to a tenth of the honey was in favor. The argument for this is that it gives the land owner a direct interest in your success since it means added income for him if you do well. But with the advent of the automobile the outapiarist is less dependent upon the landowner for board for themselves and teams. In fact it very often happens that it is neither advisable nor profitable for him to loiter for an hour or two till meal time when they could easily, in the same time, return home or go to the next out-yard and commence operations. Another point is that the apiarist may want to run one year entirely for increase with no surplus crop, or another year they may have to feed heavily, when it would be no more than right that the landowner should bear their proportion of the feed given.

The cash rental is given in the largest number of instances. The amount varies greatly with the different apiarists, being as high as $50.00 in some instances and as low as .$5.00 in others, depending on the section of the country and upon the quality of the land upon which the bees are located.

In California the usual rental price for bees in the forest reserves is ten cents per colony spring count. The late E. France of Wisconsin reported in 1895 giving 25 cents per colony. In all instances it pays to be free with gifts of honey and to keep on the best of terms with the landlord.

In some instances the agreement includes that the owner shall hive all swarms, in others they are paid from 25 cents to $1.50 for each swarm hived.

We would favor a cash rental averaging probably $20.00 to $25.00 per year for each location for an apiary of 75 to 125 colonies with a cash payment of 75 cents to $1.00 for each swarm hived.

In any case the agreement should be in writing, copies to be retained both by the landlord and the beekeeper, so that there can be no question later as to terms agreed upon. We give below a standard form for such an agreement which can be altered to suit specific conditions.

This article of agreement made and entered into this day of,_____ 20___, by and between party of_____ the first part and _____party of the second part, witnessed:

That in consideration of one dollar in hand paid by the said second party and the stipulations and agreements hereinafter mentioned, said first party hereby agrees to lease to the said second party, the following lands to wit _____acres in the part of their home place, for a period of___ years.

It is hereby mutually agreed that the said land shall be used as an apiary site and for no other purpose except as may be necessary in the care of the bees and the production and marketing of honey and wax.

The second party hereby agrees to pay to the first party the sum of _____dollars annually on or before the first of July as rental for said premises, with an additional rental of _____ pounds of honey each season that the total production of honey from said apiary reaches two Hundred pounds or more

Said second party agrees to build a suitable fence to protect said apiary from live stock at their own expense and to keep same in repair during the life of the agreement.

It is further agreed that the said second party shall have access to said premises by way of an already established road: that they shall have the privilege of erecting buildings thereon for their own use in connection with the said apiary and that such buildings shall remain the property of the second party and they shall retain the right to remove the same at any time that they shall have occasion to do so.

Signed in duplicate this____day of 20_____.

Signed _____

Signed _____

It may not be amiss to give form of agreement suitable for running of bees on shares, where it is even more desirable to have an absolute agreement between the two contracting parties. The agreement may vary with the conditions. We give below the usual share agreement where the bees are owned by one party and run by another on the share basis.

This agreement made on this first day of December 2015, by and between John Smith and Stephen Brown, witnessed: That the said John Smith hereby agrees to lease to Stephen Brown 50 colonies of bees together with hives and equipment and to furnish such extra supers as may be necessary to harvest the crop, for the season of 2016.

The said Stephen Brown agrees to give prompt and careful attention to said bees, to use clue care to guard against disease, and if disease be found at any time to give proper treatment therefor; to use diligence in saving all swarms that may issue, to provide necessary stores for needy colonies, and to perform all other necessary labor in the harvesting of the honey crop and attending to the usual work of the apiary. At the close of the season they further agree to return to John Smith the full number of colonies provided with sufficient stores for the coming winter, provided, however, that they shall not be responsible for losses caused by tornadoes, storms or other causes beyond their control, and provided also that in case of honey dearth and short crop necessitating feeding, such sugar as required is to be supplied by the said John Smith.

It is further mutually agreed that all surplus honey and wax shall be divided equally between John Smith and Stephen Brown, and that each shall furnish the necessary containers for their portion; also that all increase shall be likewise equally divided and that each shall furnish one-half the necessary hives therefor, and that the said Stephen Brown shall furnish their own tools, provide for their own board and other expenses; that the said John Smith shall not be held liable for any expenses except as herein provided.

Signed this first day of December, 2015.

JOHN SMITH
STEPHEN BROWN

CHAPTER V

THE APIARY ITSELF

Depending upon the permanency of the apiary, the beekeeper will look after its arrangement with more or less detail. It is best to have order and tidiness, in fact the work can usually be done with less labor if order is observed, but as stated before in outapiary work it is inadvisable to be so exacting in neatness as to make the overhead expense out of proportion to the corresponding gain.

Fig. 12. The favorite way is to place the colonies in long rows facing the same direction.

Arrangement

Depending upon the system and desire of each individual apiarist, the hives may be arranged in rows several feet apart

Fig. 13. The hives may be placed in rows facing each other.

facing in the same direction, in rows back to back, or in groups of two, three or five as the case may be. But the apiarist should give this matter due consideration with the ultimate object of making a saving of steps and labor. Too much regularity may cause loss of queens in wedding flight and it is well to have trees, bushes, etc., to mark the location.

Number of Colonies

The number of colonies which may be kept in an apiary will vary with each location and is dependent entirely upon the honey resources of the locality and the number of bees in that immediate vicinity which will share the crop.

Fig. 14. The Scholl apiaries in Texas are arranged in groups of five.

Adam Grimm, writing in the American Bee Journal in 1874 said: "There is no question with me any longer that the smaller the number of colonies kept in one location, the greater the yield of honey from a single colony. But the question is not how the beekeeper can secure the largest yield of honey from a smaller number of colonies, but how can they secure the largest income by keeping bees."

Grimm thought that for their locations in Wisconsin the ideal number was from 50 to 100 colonies placed at least three miles apart.

Alexander of New York was able to keep 750 colonies in one yard and one year secured an average per colony production of 141 pounds of extracted honey. It is certain, however, that this yield was phenomenal, and was due to an extremely fortunate location and to a profusion of bloom from spring to fall.

It falls upon each beekeeper to determine for themselves, either by experience or by excellent foresight for just how many colonies each locality will afford nectar with the greatest amount of profit, not forgetting that the poor seasons must be considered along with the good ones.

John W. Cash of Northern Georgia, a very successful apiarist, found that the number, for him, is not to exceed forty colonies,

Fig. 15. John W. Cash of Georgia finds that forty colonies in an apiary is about the limit in their locality.

while J. J. Wilder of Southern Georgia estimates fifty the maximum. In most eastern and central western locations, successful apiarists keep from 75 to 125 colonies, the number being larger as we get into the Rocky Mountain region and the Pacific Coast, always being dependent on the nectar possibilities of each location and the number of other bees to share the pasturage.

I have found that in the Midwest, because of current farming practices it is unadvised to place more than 20 colonies in one location. Gone are days of past.

Decoy Hives

Many outapiarists practice with success, the placing of decoy hives in elevated places throughout the apiary to catch a portion of the swarms which may come out during the absence of the beekeeper. Others so manipulate their hives that the swarms issuing are negligible in quantity and not worthy of special arrangements.

Fig, 16. The California apiary often contains two or three hundred colonies without overstocking. The above is reproduction of one of M. H. Mendleson's apiaries.

Watering Places

Water is necessary for bees, and unless it is naturally plentiful near the apiary, the bees will find it where they can. Much annoyance will be saved near-neighbors around horse and chicken troughs if the beekeeper will provide in the apiary sufficient to supply the bees and brood during a drought.

Different devices are used for this, probably the most common being a tub or half-barrel with the water covered with an abundance of small sticks or cork chips. If the barrel is placed under the eaves of the honey-house it may be replenished without effort on the part of the apiarist.

Solar Wax Extractors

Wax scrapings and bits of comb should be saved, and there is no better way than to have installed in each permanent outapiary a wax solar extractor which will take care of bits of comb thrown in and will, at the same time, provide safe resting place for odds and ends of comb in which there are small quantities of honey.

Fig. 17, A watering place should be provided to keep the bees away from the horse and chicken troughs.

Fig. 18. A three-deck watering trough in use by a large queen-breeder in the South.

Fire

We have known of whole apiaries being swept by fire and totally destroyed through lack of foresight or negligence on the part of their owner, to make proper safeguards before a drought. It is time well spent to have your apiary in such shape that fire cannot spread. Besides, weeds in the apiary serve no good purpose. They hinder the flight of the bees if left in front of the hives.

Extra Supplies

Extra hives, supers, etc., at each apiary are within the discretion of the apiarist. It is, however, a good plan to have smoker, veils, hive tool, a few hives, and a few supers ready at hand in case they are needed.

Many apiarists establish honey-houses and full outfits for extracting at each yard. While these are not absolutely necessary, we consider them of sufficient importance to warrant a special chapter on honey-houses.

M.G. Dadant

CHAPTER VI

GENERAL SYSTEMS OF MANAGEMENT

With every beekeeper will lay the task of determining their specific system of management. Each one will have peculiarities of management which will affect the general system they will follow in their outapiaries. Moreover, financial and other considerations may have a bearing in determining just which of the following systems they will consider a model.

The Permanent Apiary

Probably a large percentage of outapiarists establish their out-yards with some degree of permanency, and most of these have honey-houses at each out-yard to take care of supers and equipment and in which to do the extracting.

Many of these have a full equipment at each yard so that the only hauling is new equipment, feed, etc. and the bringing in of the extracted crop. However, having extracting equipment at each yard means much idle capital during a large portion of the year. Moreover, such equipment is likely to suffer more from neglect than from use.

Likely a larger proportion have a portable extracting equipment, thus requiring less capital. The extractor, uncapping cans, melter, etc., are carried from apiary to apiary, the honey usually being hauled home as fast as extracted.

Shifting Apiaries and the Portable System

In many regions it, is inadvisable to establish on so permanent a basis, and the beekeepers place their out-yards without any provision for housing equipment except temporary shelter for supers, etc. Extracting, in these instances, is done in a tent, in a light, quickly erected and quickly transported house of screen or of muslin, or in a portable house on wheels. This plan is practiced in all parts of the country, but lends itself to existing conditions best in California and other extreme western locations, where migratory beekeeping is popular.

Migratory Beekeeping

The older reader, when migratory beekeeping is mentioned, will recall more especially the experiences of C. 0. Perrine and others in attempting to practice migratory beekeeping between the North and the South, a long haul, fraught with large chances of failure, and usually proven so unsuccessful as to leave no doubt as to the inefficiency of the idea.

But the advent of the automobile and truck has made a uniform success of migratory beekeeping on a short haul, say of 100 miles or less. Many central western beekeepers now haul their bees from the clover fields to the river bottoms in fall to catch the honey from heartsease and Spanish needle. In California it allows opportunity to go to the orange groves, then to the bean fields, to the sage and alfalfa, or to another crop in reach of the beekeeper.

Some beekeepers, in fact, have had success in carload shipments from California to Nevada and Utah and back, and recent successes were reported of shipments to Utah and Wyoming by Texas beekeepers during their seasons of drought and dearth in 1916 and 1917.

Migratory beekeeping on hauls of 100 miles or less may be considered a success, but long trans-continental hauls will need an experienced beekeeper who is readily able to incur losses sustained by unfortunate occurrences which are to be expected with this plan in too great frequency, and who knows the ins and outs of moving bees on a large scale.

The Central Plant

An increasing number of our larger beekeepers dispense with equipment at each yard and have a central plant, all supers being stored at home, and all honey being hauled in by truck to be extracted.

This has the advantage that, in the central plant, all conveniences may be installed permanently. Many items of equipment may be added that would otherwise not be practical.

With such equipment and a central force, a larger daily average of honey can be extracted. The apiarist is usually surer of regular hours, and one set of equipment is all that is necessary.

At the end of the season, all supers are at home where they can be overhauled for the coming crop.

The disadvantages are that there is greater chance of spreading foulbrood, in fact some of the champions of this system would not use it were foulbrood prevalent in their vicinity. There is some danger to run from melting or breaking the heavy combs while hauling them, and, moreover, roads must be good enough for your truck to travel.

In hauling the sticky combs back to the apiaries, robbing is likely to occur. Then, too, if some of your apiaries are 30 or 40 miles away the long haul may increase trucking costs possibly to the point of overbalancing the advantages.

If bees are cellar-wintered, cellars will be needed at the outyard in addition.

Probably a large proportion of beginners will do well to establish out-yards with some provision for extracting there until the central system can be applied directly to their needs through experience. It would be difficult in most instances to get a large beekeeper who has used the central plant to go back to the older method.

Keeping Records

Probably in no branch of beekeeping do we find such a diversity in methods as in the keeping of records of individual colonies. Likely the most minute and most efficient system would be a card index with a card for each colony, properly subdivided to record each operation. Close records may also be kept by record books. Systems of colored pegs, signs, discs, etc., placed on the hives or beside them are also used with success.

Fig. 19. Rough records on the back of hive caps are used by many large producers.

Probably a great proportion of large beekeepers keep only partial records of colonies, using a "rough and ready" system, while some use no records at all. It is advisable to have records sufficient to trace the progress of disease, the age of queens and the honey producing qualities of all colonies.

Extensive records are hardly practical for the outapiarist. That is why we see, in increasing numbers, the use of indelible crayon, blue pencil, etc., on the inside of hive cover or on the back of the hive. Such marks will last a year or two before they are obliterated by the weather, only to be replaced by newer records by the beekeeper.

Michael Palmer of Vermont uses duct tape and a permanent marker to write on it on each hive. This method makes record keeping at each hive easy and instant. Then after the outapiary is worked you can transfer those notes to your permanent record book.

CHAPTER VII

WINTER AND SPRING WORK

If their bees have been properly prepared for winter the outapiarist will have little to occupy him in the apiary except to see that bees in cellars are wintering properly or that entrances are free from ice if they practice out-of-door wintering. This can usually be arranged in co-operation with the farmer at whose place the bees are kept so that numerous trips to the outapiary will hardly be necessary.

First Examination

As soon as the bees have a good cleansing flight in spring and a moderate spell of weather seems imminent, it will be well for the beekeeper to make the first round of their out-yards. Entrances should be freed of the accumulations of winter, dead bees if any cleaned out, alighting boards made clear, and all dead colonies carefully closed so as to prevent the robbing of their honey.

It is to be hoped that the outapiarist does not have American foulbrood to fight, but if they have, and a case has, through oversight or neglect, been allowed to go into winter quarters, the colony's death during winter without consequent closing up in early spring will in all probability give the beekeeper much trouble through spread of the infection by robbing.

It is true that these same combs may be used later by the beekeeper in making divisions, but in such instances they will only be given to one or two colonies and if proper records are kept such disease may be easily traced.

At this examination it will pay to regulate the entrance of each colony commensurate with its strength, reducing the weak or queenless to a very small bee space and enlarging the entrance of the stronger colonies.

Feed should be at hand to replenish such as have run short through one cause or another.

Many apiarists practice leveling hives on this first round. It may be advisable, however, to delay this until later when all settling of the ground will have ceased from winter heaving.

Second Examination

The first examination, of necessity, will be superficial owing to its earliness. One should be wary of disturbing the cluster to look for stores, queens, or disease. This may well be attempted however, on the second trip which will be made as soon as settled weather has arrived.

Drone-Layers and Queenless Colonies

In a majority of instances it will not pay to spend valuable time on drone-laying or queenless colonies. It is with difficulty that queens are secured at this season and such colonies generally are very hard to get queen-right. Probably the best procedure is to unite all such colonies by Dr. Miller's newspaper plan. This may also be advisable with weak queen-right colonies. These may profitably be united with drone-layers after the drone-laying queen has first been found and disposed of. In a majority of instances, however, it will be more profitable to unite a drone-layer or a queenless colony with another strong and queen-right colony rather than unite several weaker colonies .

Feeding---Spring Dwindling

If the beekeeper has been foresighted, they will so have prepared their colonies for winter that little feeding will have to be done in the spring, since one of the principles of successful wintering is ample stores in the fall.

Fig. 20. The ordinary ten-pound friction-top pail with one or two holes in the cover may be used as a stimulative feeder.

In a similar manner, if proper preparations were taken the fall before, the bugaboo of "spring dwindling" will usually itself "dwindle" to insignificance. A young queen, ample stores, and plenty of young bees in the late fall are the best cures for dwindling in spring outapiary or home yard.

Building up ---Stimulative Feeding

The main factor in spring management, of course, is to have all colonies built up to maximum strength for the main honey flow, whether it be for the orange blossom of California or the white clover of Iowa.

Fig. 21. Five-gallon oil cans are excellent for hauling feed to the outyard

Ordinarily we would expect best results where there is a natural building up through the use of abundant natural stores. But in many cases this is not sufficient.

Natural pollen, in rare instances may be lacking, and the out-apiarist may have to provide a substitute. Lack of water may also hinder brood rearing, though this is rarely so in early spring.

Uncapping of sealed honey to induce the bees to use up such stores in brood rearing is practiced by some, but this would hardly be advisable in the outapiary. Nor would stimulative feeding, which consists of giving a small quantity of warm syrup to each colony at intervals to simulate a natural flow. B. A. Aldrich of Iowa uses ten pound tin pails with but a single hole in the cover for stimulation. In this manner the bees get the syrup slowly though it is not always served hot.

With excellent prospects for a clover flow, it might pay to feed for stimulation between the fruit bloom and clover so as to hold brood rearing at its highest point and reach the main flow with the largest possible number of bees. The drawbacks to stimulative feeding should, however, be weighed carefully by the apiarist as the dangers of chilling brood through over stimulation are great. Extra cost of special trips to out-yards must also be considered. Involved manipulation is necessary. Stimulative feeding is advisable mainly in locations where several weeks elapse without any bloom, after first bloom.

Foulbrood

With the coming of the first flow in spring it is essential that all colonies be examined for foulbrood. Some localities are still free from the disease, but we never know when it may appear in our own yards from causes without. In spring a case of American foulbrood develops rapidly, because the bees are then using up the faulty stores for their brood, the colony quickly dwindles, and the stores, if any, are left at the mercy of the robbers who all too quickly transmit the disease to their own young. Here again the value of contraction of the entrance of weak colonies is evident, since it gives the weak foulbrood colonies opportunity to protect themselves until such a time as the beekeeper can give proper treatment.

With European as with American foulbrood the time to examine colonies and treat them is as early in spring as possible. Proper treatment before or at the beginning of the first flow often may result in subsequent building up of the colony for flows to follow.

The Hospital Yard

A number of outapiarists practice with success the assembling of all colonies with American foulbrood into a single yard for treatment. This has advantages which I believe overbalance the disadvantages.

In the first place, one of the dangers of shaking for foulbrood in the out-yard is the chance of bees drifting to neighboring colonies with full honey sacs, thus possibly transmitting the disease. Manipulations in the out-yard are necessarily hurried. Proper care, desirable in correct treatment, may not be given.

If the hospital yard is to be established, it should by all means be placed in or near the home yard. Here the best of care may be taken and the necessity of extra-long trips avoided. F. W Hall of Iowa has practiced this plan for several years and finds it very satisfactory.

Varrora Treatment

Spring time is the best time to get varrora in check. If fall treatments were effective then spring time treatments might not necessarily be required. The outapiarist should check a select number of hives in each out-yard and if the economic threshold for treatment is met then treatment before the main flow is advised.

To keep a colony full of varrora in an out-yard is ill advised due to that hives possibility of crashing between visits and the remaining hives robbing it out and carrying an increased mite load to their hives.

Since varrora treatments are forever changing due to the mites building resistance it is beyond this author to recommend a certain treatment. And since there are also many different views on whether to treat or not will be left to each individual beekeeper.

I have always tried to take the very best care of my livestock an find it odd that a beekeeper would not do everything possible to make sure their stock not only survives but thrives. A hive full of varrora not only will not live it will also not thrive and produce a bountiful crop for the beekeeper.

CHAPTER VIII

EARLY SUMMER WORK

The outapiarist now approaches the season which is of greatest importance in determining whether their efforts towards keeping more bees, and in scattered locations, are to be successful. They must be able to so manipulate that their colonies will, in a large measure, remain intact for the flows which are to follow. Faulty manipulation with consequent swarming, may mean a lessening of the crop to the extent that they will work at a loss, while intense management may result either in not being able to care for all the bees handled or increase operating expenses beyond the returns.

Swarm Control

Your method of management may call for examination of colonies periodically to cut out queen-cells, and to keep all queens clipped to prevent swarms leaving, but this entails a large amount of extra work at a time when the outapiarist is busiest caring for their numerous yards.

Even though the above method is practiced, the mere fact that all queens are clipped will not prevent the desire on the part of the bees to swarm, nor will it prevent an effort to swarm, with subsequent loss of time in honey production.

What we should strive for is to so manipulate the out-yards that we may keep the impulse to swarm at the minimum, for with any system of management a protracted flow may result in a small percentage of swarming. We should endeavor to make this percentage negligible.

Six requisites have been emphasized by C. P. Dadant as desirable to control swarming. They are a minimum of drone comb, ample breeding room, plenty of super room for honey, shade for hives, ample ventilation, and young queens.

Drone Comb

The use of full sheets of foundation, both in the brood chamber and in super frames, has to a large extent done away with super-abundance of drone comb in the hive. Occasionally however, carelessness in inserting foundation and improper wiring, resulting in sagging, will cause considerable drone comb. It will pay well either to cut all drone comb from defective frames and insert worker comb or foundation in its place, or discard such combs completely.

Large Breeding Chamber

More and more, extensive beekeepers are inclining towards the hive with the large brood chamber, especially for extracted honey production; a hive in which the queen is unrestricted in laying, which will accommodate the most prolific breeding queens.

Many outapiarists using the ten-frame or even the eight-frame Langstroth hive expand the brood chamber by adding a second story for the queen as soon as the first one restricts her laying powers. Their plan, then, is to restrict the queen again to the lower story at the beginning of the first good flow by means of the queen excluder using the Demaree plan or some other with modifications to insure the largest possible breeding room under existing conditions.

This again calls for considerable manipulation, much more than is necessary when the brood chamber has, in one story, the necessary breeding room.

Shade for the Outapiary

Shade is provided in the outapiary in several manners; by means of shade trees, extra roofs on each hive, or in some sections by "ramadas" mentioned elsewhere in this book. Care should be taken not to have too dense shade or there is a possibility of encroaching too much on ventilation which is treated below as one of the requisites we are seeking.

Ventilation

There is nothing which will more quickly induce bees to cluster out. sulk, and get the swarming fever than a total disregard of ventilation. How many an amateur or "backwoods" beekeeper reckons the working qualities of their bees by the number clustered at the entrance. How many, too, are sure that this is a sign that the bees are going to swarm. Who cannot recall the inevitable cluster on the outside of the poorly-ventilated box-hive on a hot summer day.

As one prominent beekeeper, James Heddon, said, "beekeeping is a business of details; "and the entrance, as it affects ventilation, is not the least of these.

Beginning in early spring when the entrance should be expanded to suit the needs of the growing colony, the outapiarist should keep well ahead of their bees, giving at length a full width entrance then adding to the ventilation either by reversing the bottom board or by raising the body of the hive from its bottom-board. In the height of a honey flow and during intense heat a two inch entrance in front or a one inch entrance all around is not excessive.

Proper spacing of frames in the hive will also give added ventilation. It is only recently that the value of a 1 ½ inch spacing of frames has been acknowledged as superior to the stereotyped 1 3/8 inch spacing which most of factory-made hives today have. The 1 1\2 inch spacing provides a larger hive not in brood area but in ventilation.

Young Queens

If we have followed recommendations on preparing our bees for winter, we will have young and vigorous queens heading all our colonies for the honey flow the following spring. But it must be remembered that there is no orthodox rule applying to the desirability of young queens. Some may prove their worthlessness before their progeny has had a chance to demonstrate harvesting ability and these should be gotten rid of at the earliest moment regardless of season.

But it is evident that the desire to swarm is generally stronger in colonies headed by old queens, so that queens less than two years old are desirable.

It may be that a queen has proven so good, her bees have been such good honey gatherers, that we have more to gain by retaining her, even though we run the risk of swarming.

There is another matter which should have some bearing on queen supersedure, and that is whether or not the queen has been through a long, heavy honey flow. In the season of crop failure, with breeding restricted, the laying qualities of a queen are not put to so severe a test, so that possibly a majority of the more prolific may be valuable enough to be retained for another season.

We cannot leave this subject without mentioning the pain of one prominent Iowa apiarist to get young queens for the harvest and thus control swarming.

At the beginning of the honey flow, (clover is their main flow), the colonies are carefully gone over and all queens over two years old killed. Each colony is properly marked as to which are desirable to breed from.

On the next examination, ten days later, all cells are destroyed and instead is inserted a comb either with a cell or a grafted cell from one of the choice breeding colonies. Again, a week or more later, the third examination makes sure that all queens have been hatched and mated, cells being inserted where needed from colonies previously prepared.

Supers and Supering

"Anticipation brings Realization." This is certainly true in putting on supers. If the outapiarist waits till the main harvest is on at home to begin their round of supering at the out-yards it is a safe guess that they will be too late at some one of their outapiaries.

Conditions would be ideal, certainly, were it possible to have all colonies ready at the same time. This may in part be attempted by equalizing brood between colonies as is practiced by some. This calls for more manipulation.

The first supers for surplus should be put on at or shortly before the opening of the honey flow. This should be before the queen becomes restricted in her egg-laying through congestion of honey in the brood chamber. Certainly it is not a wise plan to add supers three weeks in advance of their need, since the bees have an added story to keep warm during the cool weather of spring. But it would be more desirable to have the supers on a week early than a week late.

So with the second and third supers, they should be given as required before the bees become crowded for storing room, while in rapid heavy flows two or even three supers may be added at once, they being filled with nectar almost as quickly as one.

Adding another super when the one below is about half full, or when the bees are storing honey from one edge of the super to the other is the usual procedure. This, of course is to be varied with the time of the flow. Toward the close of the flow it will be wiser to crowd the bees rather than add extra supers which may not be needed. This is especially true in fall flows when we wish to crowd the brood chamber for winter and when there is very little chance of inducing swarming by such crowding.

The number of supers which are necessary per hive vary with the system adopted by each beekeeper. If they intend to extract during the flow they can get along with less supers. More and more, outapiarists are practicing the plan of having on hand enough drawn supers to hold the crop of an ordinary flow. Then if the season is bountiful it may be necessary to extract in the middle of the harvest. The Dadant apiaries are run with from three to five, six inch depth, Dadant size supers per colony. This will hold the average crop. Yet in 1910 it was necessary to keep continually extracting to stay ahead of the bees. One apiary was extracted four times during the honey flow.

It is possible to get along with two supers per hive, with careful manipulation, but four or even six would be much better.

Queen Excluders

Many beekeepers running for extracted honey use queen excluders to keep the queen from laying in the surplus cases. There are two objections to their use. In the first place they hinder to some extent the free passage of the bees into the supers above. In the second place they restrict the queen and are apt to induce swarming.

In hives with a large brood chamber the excluder is not so necessary, since the queen has sufficient room below and finds no occasion to go above, and with the use of shallow supers in connection with the large brood chamber, queen excluders become unnecessary except in rare instances.

To overcome this objection of queen restriction in the smaller hives many beekeepers practice the Demaree plan or a modification thereof. Until the beginning of the surplus flow the queen is allowed the use of two brood chambers for egg laying. Immediately after the flow starts, she is put into the lower body with a frame or two of brood, the balance of the body being filled with drawn combs or foundation and an excluder is inserted between the two bodies. Thus she is supplied for a considerable time with breeding room. If this be repeated at intervals the queen may be supplied with empty combs and the danger of brood restriction removed.

In the greater number of instances, however, the excluder when once placed is left for the remainder of the flow. An increasing number of beekeepers use the excluder till most of the danger of swarming is over, when it is removed and a super of sealed honey placed next to the brood chamber to keep the queen from going above.

As stated above, the use of shallow extracting supers discourages the queen from going above, especially if such combs are spaced far apart, putting eight, or at most nine combs in a ten frame super. Mr. Chambers of Arizona claims success in putting but eight frames in a regular ten-frame full depth super to keep the queen below.

However, we must not lose sight of the fact that all such plans as tend to restrict the laying of the queen are not as desirable as those which give her sufficient room, nor do they have as much effect in the prevention of swarming.

CHAPTER IX

THE HARVEST

If the beekeeper has sufficient super room for the full crop, there will be no trouble. All honey may be removed at the end of the season. But if we must extract during the honey flow, care is necessary to get only ripe honey, or if any unripe is removed, to place it in open tanks to allow evaporation.

As a general rule, when extracting during the flow, it will not be safe to extract any but sealed honey . However, here also the beekeeper must use their own discretion. Very often they can tell whether the honey will do by its density, by the readiness with which it may or may not be shaken from the combs.

Removing the Honey

The modern bee-escape is a most useful appliance in removing honey. It is almost, indispensable to the comb-honey producer. Since the use of the automobile has become so common, the escape has enhanced in value to the extracted honey person as well. It is but a short trip, nowadays, to the outapiary in the afternoon, putting on the escapes so that the extracting may go on in full force the next morning. In an hour or two, two men can place sufficient escapes for a full day's work for four men, but care must be taken in placing these escapes, especially if there is a dearth of honey, not to allow openings in the supers where robbers may find their way to the unprotected honey. This will not only develop a serious case of robbing but may also mean the complete emptying of such supers as are exposed.

The presence of brood in the supers hinders materially the effectiveness of the bee-escape. Similarly, if the queen happens to be in the super, the bees will not desert her to go below. These two causes have many tunes resulted in failure and rejection of the escape when with care it would have worked properly. Bees will also leave sealed honey much more readily than unsealed Many remove but one super at a time with the escape, but the writer has experienced but small chances of failure when removing two, three or four supers with one escape, and this is our usual procedure.

The greatest hindrance to the escape is very cool weather when the bees are less apt to run down. They do go down, at least, very slowly. Another objection in cool weather is that when the bees go down, the honey cools quickly and when taken off is very stiff and cold and hard to uncap and extract.

Many use no escapes, thus saving themselves an extra trip to the outapiary. They use a combination of smoking and brushing to rid the combs of bees, driving them below with cautious smoking, after which the remaining ones may be readily brushed. The bristle bee brush is best for this purpose. Carbolic cloths are spread over supers by some to drive the bees down.

The advantage of the bee-escape, however, cannot be denied, much overbalancing its disadvantages.

Each outapiarist has their own method of getting full supers from the apiary to the extracting house. Some erect tracks with cars capable of loading several supers at a time. Larger majorities locate the houses as conveniently as possible and use an ordinary garden wheelbarrow equipped with springs to lessen the jar on the combs.

It is wise to be provided with burlap cloths to be used as robber cloths to cover supers from the time they are taken from the hives until they are in the shelter of the extracting building. A flat drip pan on the barrow is almost a necessity, especially where bees are brushed instead of using the bee-escape.

The advent of the bee blower allows quick and easy removal of bees from the supers. The stand is set up in front of each hive and as supers are placed on it the bees are blown out in front of the hive. This quick removal allows a team of two or three to quickly remove supers from a whole outapiary.

The use of a fume board and chemicals are another quick and easy way to drive the bees from the supers. With today's pleasant smelling chemicals the bees are quickly driven from the supers. This method is the one I prefer over the others. While the fume boards are on one set of hives I can remove the supers quickly from the ones they were on.

Extracting

The manner of extracting must vary greatly with the system of the outapiarist, whether they have a hand portable outfit, a permanent equipment at each yard, or hauls all honey to the central plant, and whether they use a crew of men or practices the one-person system. The idea may be to work as rapidly as possible with a large crew, or take time and reduce outside labor to a minimum. Extractors will be taken up further in another chapter dealing with extracting houses and equipment.

Replacing Supers

There is some advantage in extracting before the close of the honey flow. In fact it will pay the apiarist to make a careful study of the honey flora and the honey flow and so time their operations that the extracting may be done just as the flow is ending, lose no honey, and still not be extracting during a honey dearth.

During a honey flow the supers may be returned to the hives as fast as extracted, the same number being replaced on each colony as it had before.

But in a honey dearth robbing will certainly be aggravated. It is better to wait till the close of the day when all supers may be returned in a short time. All can then be cleaned by the colonies before morning. For carrying supers back to the apiary a hand barrow is very desirable. Two men can carry from ten to twenty supers at a load while one person in the apiary smokes the bees and replaces equipment.

Some beekeepers practice setting freshly extracted supers out in the open for the bees to clean up at will. In most cases this is very objectionable and not to be recommended. Robbing is encouraged and danger of infection, should any foulbrood be present, is great.

Fig. 22. The placing of wet' combs in piles in the open for bees to rob out and cleanup is to be discouraged.

Fig. 23. The France honey strainer is cylindrical and will fit directly into the honey-tank.

If the supers are to be replaced after the last flow in the fall, when the weather is cool, each strong colony may be given four, five or even six supers to clean and guard, thus making easier work in removing the supers later. Several good beekeepers do not replace supers after the last extracting but hold them until needed the next spring. N. E. France of Wisconsin has many times carried such wet supers through the next summer and states that they are much less likely to be injured by moth than the dry supers.

Fig.24. The Dadant strainer for barrels.

However, an objection is that these wet supers may be needed before the crop the following spring, for increase or otherwise, when the dry super may be used with little robbing whereas the wet one may necessitate ceasing operations in a whole apiary. There may also be a chance of honey souring in the wet combs, if any fermentation is present.

Receptacles for the Crop

Sometimes a major portion of the honey is placed in cans as fast as it comes from the extractor, though it is evidently only a makeshift way. It is impossible to remove all impurities in so short a time no matter how careful the strainer. But the apiary not permanently located, where all work is done with a portable outfit cannot install settling tanks for a single run, neither is it advantageous to haul the honey home and re-empty it. One prominent Wisconsin beekeeper, however, has provided himself with a number of large size milk cans. The honey is strained into these at the outapiary and transferred to the settling tank at home after each day's run. They find the plan very satisfactory.

The ideal method, of course, is to have permanently installed settling tanks and enough of them to hold the extracting until the honey is well settled. This can best be done with the central extracting system where all supers are handled at home. It is also practiced to some extent with permanent out-yards where buildings are well equipped. The Edson Apiaries in California have 2 or 3 ton settling tanks. The honey settles overnight and is drawn into 5 gallon cans the next morning when it is stored in warehouses at the station nearest the out-yard at which they are working.

Honey Knives

The steam-heated honey knife has won its way to favor with a large majority of the best beekeepers. Its advantages are most marked when the honey is thick, the weather cool, and uncapping difficult. It can be dispensed with when extracting is done in hot weather and uncapping is comparatively easy. It is the thing for the inexperienced person, while it may be used only in the emergency by the expert with the cold knife. The chief uncapper for the Dadant apiaries made a record of uncapping solidly sealed combs in shallow frames at the rate of 1000 pound* of honey per hour on a half day run. He did it with a cold knife. Yet they realize the advantage of the hot knife and never neglect to have it along for the emergency.

Fig. 25. Large settling tanks for storing honey, previous to drawing into proper receptacles.

Cappings and Capping Melters

Unfortunately one or two large beekeepers in the past have recommended the use of barrels for cappings, a few holes being bored in the barrel for honey drainage when the rest of the mass would be hauled home for disposition. I can conceive of no worse method of caring for the cappings than by the use of such barrels or cans. I have in mind one shipment of cappings so barreled and sent to a big comb-rendering plant to be melted up. Five barrels in the shipment weighed in the neighborhood of 1500 pounds. At least two thirds of this was honey, yet the beekeeper by their methods was unable to get out more honey, and the rest was to be wasted.

Although my preference is for the capping can or capping box, a large number of the best beekeepers would not work without the capping melter though they realize its shortcomings. Evident it is, that it provides the easiest and quickest methods of disposing of the cappings, turning them on the spot into honey and wax, and it is especially valuable for the one person plant.

Its disadvantages are that it is hot to work over in summer, and it discolors the honey and injures its flavor, since it is impossible to apply sufficient heat to melt the wax without great danger of slightly scorching the honey. Cappings from old combs in which brood has been reared, melt more slowly and cause the most trouble in scorching. Some claim that this small amount of discolored honey when added to the day's extracting mixes so readily as to be unobserved in either color, taste or smell by any observer. We are inclined to doubt this. The essential oils from the bloom, which give the finest flavor, are easily evaporated. Another criticism of the melter is that it makes added equipment when used in connection with the portable outfit. It would work best with the central plant.

Probably one of the chief reasons for dislike of the capping can or box lies in the fact that the best manner of procedure is not always used. Explanation can probably be given by describing in detail the plan used in the Dadant apiaries which is used similarly by many beekeepers.

As portable extracting equipment is used in connection with a permanent honey house, and in this equipment is included a 24-inch capping can capable of holding usually the cappings of a good day's run. Every hour or so during the day, time enough is taken to give these cappings a thorough stirring and breaking up with a strong stick so that the honey may more readily drain. Honey drains off so freely that it has to be emptied from below both noon and night and sometimes more often. The cappings are therefore pretty well drained when the time comes to load for home in the evening, when the full can is taken along. It is left to drain overnight. In the morning the cappings are transferred to a larger tank with but a shallow space at the bottom for the collection of the balance of the honey. When the end of the season and a slack time come, this dried mass may be run through a melter if desired. The cappings of the 1918 fall extracting in the Dadant apiaries from 11,000 pounds of honey were, for a test, run through a separating can and melter fashioned after those of Sechrist and Crane. Less than sixty pounds of honey were secured from the whole lot.

P. W. Sowinski, of Michigan, running a one man plant, uses the uncapping box, spreading the cappings evenly over the box during the day's run. At evening he rolls up his sleeves and thoroughly breaks up and mixes these cappings until all is a conglomerated mass. By morning the cappings are practically dry.

Fig. 26. Box arranged for holding supers of combs while they are being sulphured from below.

Danger of Moths

With varying crop conditions the apiarist may have hives and supers of combs without protection of bees when danger of moths comes. All such should be watched carefully at two week periods and proper methods to destroy moths applied, should they be necessary. The worst damage comes, naturally, in the late summer, after successive broods have hatched out and joined forces. Carbon disulphid and Sulphur are both used with success.

Combs which have been without protection of bees during cold weather, in northern states are in slight danger, if properly closed to exclude moths when warm weather arrives.

Fig. 27. . A cylindrical honey-house made especially for storing combs by hanging them in racks so the moths will not enter them, and also for using sulphur fumes. Apiary of H. C. Cook of Omaha.

Those on which bees have wintered will have to be watched carefully from early spring, especially those of colonies that have died in early spring.

One beekeeper so built their honey house that the rafters are spaced for hanging combs between them. Such combs, isolated and exposed to the light, run small chance of being moth-eaten.

Today sulphur fuming of comb is not recommended. Instead of Sulphur todays beekeeper uses para-moth crystals for protection of the comb.

Supers are stacked approximately ten high and para-moth crystals are placed on a paper plate on top of the super stack. The supers are then either wrapped in stretch film or all cracks are taped up. Periodically the stacks are checked and the crystals are replaced as they evaporate.

Care must be taken in the spring to ensure the supers are aired out for a few days with no crystals in them or else the hive will be killed as they are placed on the hive.

Keeping your comb from the wax-moth is probably one of the most economical things that a beekeeper can do. Great amounts of honey can be stored if the bees don't have to rebuild comb year after year. Protect your drawn comb, as it is your most valuable asset.

Foulbrood

Second and third examinations may be necessary when the locality has foulbrood. European foulbrood should largely have disappeared with the honey-flow if proper steps were taken at its inception. American foulbrood may appear at any time and the beekeeper cannot be too careful in searching it out. A diseased colony detected and destroyed or treated late in summer or fall may save many in the spring.

Requeening

Probably most of the requeening is done after the main spring honey-flow. It is desirable to carry out such requeening in the outapiary in a wholesale manner to avoid unnecessary trips. Such requeening should also be done, where possible, during a light flow, when chances of successful introduction are best.

As prominent a beekeeper as the late Wm. McEvoy practiced requeening each summer, others requeen every other year, while others requeen only when absolutely necessary, leaving it to the bees generally to supersede a poor queen when the time comes. More and more the tendency is to requeen at least every other year.

With the desirability of a full colony of young bees for wintering, requeening should be completed in time to insure it.

CHAPTER X

FALL AND EARLY WINTER

If the beekeeper has been forewarned, they will have, in the summer, taken precautionary measures towards getting their bees in the best possible shape in preparation for winter. The three prime requisites for successful wintering are;

1. Strong Colonies of young bees.
2. Plenty of healthful stores.
3. Ample protection from winds and cold.

It is necessary to begin preparations for the first requisite quite early in fall, since the bees must be reared in sufficient time to have the colony strong before cooler weather sets in. Lacking a honey flow, it may be necessary for the beekeeper to make a tour of out-yards, feeding stimulative to imitate a flow, so that proper breeding will take place. Inasmuch as young queens usually breed more prolifically, they are desirable.

Lacking good natural stores, it may be necessary to do fall feeding. Not a small number let this matter go till too late, instead of getting colonies heavy with honey well ahead of cold weather, and too many colonies are underfed, resulting in dwindling in spring or the necessity of intermittent feedings in early spring.

Protection from the Weather

As stated previously under the chapter on locating apiaries, it is desirable to so locate the apiary that the contour of the land, natural forestry, undergrowth, etc., may help in breaking the force of the winds. Artificial windbreaks for the apiary as a whole may also be used. But there will be required, in all northern climates at least, additional wind and cold protection for the hives individually, and such protection will serve to good purpose much farther south than yet practiced by many beekeepers in the milder zones.

The character of such protection for the outapiary will be dependent to a great extent on three things:

1. Locality and location.
2. Permanence of the apiary.
3. Plan of operations.

It will hardly be advisable for the Southern person to consider seriously the proper conditions for cellar wintering, since the amount of protection their bees need will not warrant cellar wintering at all. So with wintering in the North. Some localities may be out of range of the hardest and coldest winds. They may be so favored that the weather is tempered, allowing an occasional flight during winter. Others may be winter-bound for months at a time, so that either cellar wintering or the utmost in outdoor packing will be absolutely necessary. To this extent each beekeeper will have their own method of wintering to study out as applicable to their particular locality.

The location does not make quite so great a difference. Yet it is easy to conceive a barren plain, windswept, which will require double the winter protection of another not two miles removed, but in a small valley with hills and brush and trees as protection from the direct blasts of the North. The outapiarists may have considered carefully the two when locating. The flora of the one may more than overbalance the disadvantages of the other.

Many apiary sites are retained only from one year to another. Many arrangements for ground rental can be made but for a single season. It would be the height of folly, under such conditions, to build a permanent cellar only to move out after having used it one season. Yet the location may be so extraordinary that the beekeeper may desire to remain and winter out-of-doors in the best available manner. Possibly, with the migratory system, it will be advisable to abandon the large winter cases as too cumbersome to carry here and there with the changed location.

Where the location is owned by the apiarist with the likelihood of their remaining over a series of years, they may select what they consider the ideal manner of protection.

Yet many of our outapiarists have grown up from a small beginning, They have started their extended beekeeping with only limited capital. One may be able, for a few years at least, to winter under conditions which neither they nor the best authorities deem advisable. It may be to their advantage to evolve a system less costly until a time when, if desirable, they can afford the capital for a new system of wintering better suited to the locality.

Moreover, their system, even if they are fortunate in having all the capital desired, may demand a wintering system that will correspond. With the centrally located plant, where all honey is hauled home to be extracted, it will not be advisable to build cellars at out-yards for wintering, when the building is required for no other purpose.

Outdoor vs. Cellar Wintering

It is very difficult to define specifically just where cellar wintering is to be preferred and where outdoor wintering. It will hardly do to indicate zones with the same mean temperatures as having the same conditions applying for wintering of bees, and this because the wind protection of the two may not be the same, the humidity may be different.

We all know that the two shores of a lake may be entirely different for fruit raising, although the mean temperature may be the same. In like manner climatic conditions may govern the desirability of out-door or cellar wintering. Moderation of climate sufficient to allow of winter flights may more than offset extra winter protection in the cellar.

Roughly we may state that where your bees average two good flight days per month, with no confinement of over six weeks duration, out-of-door wintering is to be preferred, providing, of course that proper wind protection is afforded.

Certain it is that many beekeepers have turned from cellar to outdoor wintering not because their locality was more favorable to the latter, but more probably because their cellars were lacking in some essential.

Fig. 28. Hives wintering close together the whole wrapped in tar paper.

On the other hand, outdoor wintering may be practiced in so many different forms and lend itself so readily to the variability of the beekeepers themselves that it is no wonder that it is chosen by many outapiarists in preference to the less elastic cellar.

Outdoor Packing Methods

A method sometimes practiced in Colorado and other sections with similar climatic conditions is to wrap colonies in tarred paper, strawboard or other similar material. Very often this is done by; first getting the colonies closely together in a long row. Probably most of the value of this protection comes through having the hives in close proximity, though the paper wrapping has some little effect on the wind and serves to cover undesirable cracks in hives and hive-covers. It is better than no packing at all ---- much better.

Alfalfa regions seem to be among the last to realize the importance of winter protection, possibly owing to the fact that their main honey flow comes late and colonies made weak by winter, as well as those lost, may be rebuilt by the time the main flow commences. Then too, their late flow insures maximum strength colonies of young bees to withstand the winter. Yet the percentage of loss in these regions seems out of proportion to what the extra investment for winter protection would be.

Fig. 29. An apiary of chaff-packed Protection hives.

In many sections the permanently packed hive is looked upon with favor. It has the advantage of requiring no extra labor for winter protection except additional packing on the top. J. T. Dunn, of Ontario, packs their double-walled hive with cork chips instead of the usual chaff, and reports exceptional success.

Objections advanced to it are that it is cumbersome to move, and heavy to lift. It only has two inches of packing all around while recommendations are usually for six to eight inches. Often no provision is made for bottom packing.

Yet in regions where limited packing is desired, this chaff-packed hive winters with success. It is more to be desired where the apiary is permanent and little moving necessary.

Single colony outer cases have the advantage that they usually provide for heavier packing, and may be removed when desired. But they also entail added equipment for the out-yard.

Fig, 30. The single colony packing case finds many advocates.

Fig. 31. The quadruple case is best in colder latitudes where an out-door wintering system is desired.

Four Colony Cases

A method growing in favor with northern beekeepers who are so situated that cellar wintering is not to be desired is the four colony case recommended by the Department of Agriculture.

This case requires the arrangement of hives in groups of four during the summer so that the case may be placed in the fall with a minimum of disturbance to the bees. It provides for eight inches or more of packing on all sides, top and bottom, while the four colonies in one case tend to conserve the heat. In regions where bees are confined to their hives for months at a time, or where exposure is great, this manner of outdoor wintering cannot be excelled.

Fig. 32. A pile of leaves stacked in nets preparatory to being taken to the outapiary for winter packing by the Dadant method.

The Dadant and Similar Systems

Outapiaries located where it is sufficiently moderate to allow of periodical flights during winter may find it to their advantage to use a system similar to that used in the Dadant apiaries.

The first essential is abundant and cheap packing material. The Dadant apiaries are located in easy reach of woods sufficient to furnish all the forest leaves desired and at minimum expense. Experiments tend to show that this packing material is superior to straw, shavings or paper.

Fig. 33. The leaves are corded on a big truck.

Large nets about six feet square are used for gathering the leaves, one net being sufficient for packing five or six of the large Dadant colonies. Nets sufficient for a full apiary are loaded on a large truck and the trip to the outapiary made.

The deep telescope caps are filled with leaves and carefully replaced after first adjusting the straw mat above to the cluster for the cluster. For hives with the shallow cover a shallow super full of leaves is added. Two men pack and replace the caps while two more follow and pack the hives outside, packing material being about six inches thick and placed on both sides and the back, leaving the front, facing south, exposed. For holding the packing on the outside, a frame of chicken netting is used. These nets rise to the top of the telescope caps making at least four inches of packing on top and all sides except the front.

There are several advantages to this plan. First, the equipment required is reduced to a minimum; rakes, leaf nets and packing frames being all that is needed extra,. The cost of packing is light, four men packing an apiary of 100 colonies in a day besides raking fresh dry leaves.

In a locality where the sun is sufficiently warm to allow of winter flights, the front of the hive warms up and induces the bees to flight, while, if they were heavily packed as with some other systems, the interior of the hive would hardly feel the sun's heat until time of day for flight was passed. In the vicinity of Hamilton, Illinois, this method has been so successful and the percentage of loss so small that it seems inadvisable to invest more in wintering equipment requiring also additional labor. Naturally, wherever possible, all apiaries are given the best advantage of location for winter protection.

Fig. 34. The straw mat is placed next to the frames

Fig. 35. Placing the big telescope covers on the hives after filling them with leaves.

Cellar Wintering and Cellars

Protection is afforded in cellar as in outdoor wintering, the difference being that the outside protection in one ease is placed around the whole apiary while in the other it is around a single colony, two colonies, or four or more, as the case may be.

The same safeguards for winter protection are to be observed as in outdoor wintering. But there are added precautions to be taken in the cellar since the bees are confined during the whole of the winter. They will have no chances for flight and changes of temperature and extreme variations in ventilation, moisture, etc., have a greater bearing.

Fig36. The completely packed hive.

A temperature of from 45 to 52 degrees is generally regarded as the best in cellar wintering, and this should be kept as even as possible during the whole winter. A colder temperature will necessitate greater ventilation while a much higher one may hasten brood rearing and induce activity by spring that will mitigate the chance of the bees surviving the winter. Generally bees winter best in the cellar at a temperature which will keep them quietest. A low temperature will require more activity to keep up the warmth of the cluster. Have a thermometer in the cellar, find the degree at which the bees are quietest, and keep it at that.

Fig. 37. One of the France bee-cellars in Wisconsin.

In many cellars, perhaps sufficient ventilation is afforded through crevices swept by the wind or through the opening and closing of entrances into the cellar. More ventilation, as stated above, will be necessary when the temperature becomes lower, requiring activity on the part of the bees. It is well to arrange a ventilator for the cellar but this need not be over 6x6 inches and should be shielded at the top to avoid light in the repository. H. H. Selwyn of Ontario has had good success with such a ventilator. He has, in addition, a sub-ventilator coming through the floor. This pipe extends from the intake for sixty feet underground before reaching the cellar. In this way the air is tempered. No doubt also that this constant stream of earth tempered air has its effect in maintaining the temperature of the cellar at the same degree, thus combining the desirability of temperature and ventilation. One beekeeper with the same system of ventilations has installed an electrically operated fan in the upper ventilator so that with any variation inside the fan pumps the air out and draws the fresh air in to take its place till the temperature again becomes normal.

Usually cellars are built of a height from 5 1/2 to 7 feet. In figuring the amount of air space to be allowed, there should be at least twelve cubic feet for each colony and two or three times this amount is desirable.

Probably a room partitioned in a house cellar which is heated by furnace is as good a repository as can be had. It is usually dry, of even temperature, and allows readily of good ventilation either through the upward draft of air or through communication with the rest of the cellar. But the outapiarist will hardly have a home cellar large enough to accommodate all their bees, nor will the houses at their out-yards he so located that they will be able to take advantage of them.

A few years ago, not a few beekeepers practiced keeping their bees in clamps. The expense of these is small and they are especially suited to the out-yard which is not permanent and in a location where outdoor wintering is not feasible. Yet it takes a peculiar soil to be suited to wintering in clamps and we can hardly recommend this method as worthy of trial by the out-yard beekeepers. There are too many failures.

Edward G. Brown, in western Iowa, winters all of his outyards in temporary cellars which he says can be made at a cost of from 25 to 50 dollars. Mr. Brown is located where the soil stands up extremely well under all conditions. When he builds a cellar he sets four posts at the four corners, having them over four feet in the ground so they will go below the floor of the cellar. They stick above ground two feet, and the two feet above ground is boarded up to hold the dirt as it is thrown from the inside in excavating. The enclosure is now dug to a depth of four feet, the dirt thrown out against the boards adding the extra two feet in depth, making six in all. A board ceiling is made and a roof placed over all, the space between being filled with some good packing material. Mr. Brown states that he winters with only one to two per cent loss and the cellar is usually good for from three to five seasons.

Fig. 38. Apiary of Edward G. Brown in the sweet clover belt of western Iowa. Notice the cheap, under-earth cellar in the background.

If the beekeeper has a reasonably permanent situation it will be to their advantage to build a permanent cellar.

This is usually built in connection with the honey-house one roof furnishing shelter for the two. In the France apiaries, in Wisconsin, the cellars under the houses are used in the summer for honey tanks and receptacles. Thus the honey is run by gravity directly from the extractor without double handling.

In such cellars the walls are built of cement or stone and the ceilings may be plastered. unless the drainage is especially good, it will hardly be feasible to leave a dirt floor, cement being much better, unless the cellar is very dry.

Some few large beekeepers with central plants provide for wintering all of their bees in a central repository.

CHAPTER XI

MOVING BEES

With modern methods for moving bees it is possible to transport them in almost any kind of weather and at all seasons of the year. Yet it is generally preferable not to move during late fall or winter when the bees may not have a chance for a cleansing flight before the winter period. Nor is it generally advisable to move during the hottest weather, nor when hives are heavy with honey. This will avoid smothering of bees and breakage or melting down of combs.

Ideal conditions for moving are to have colonies light in stores, fairly light in brood, thus giving chance for best ventilation. Cool weather, in early or late spring, when bees hardly fly, is best. If the weather is hot, take advantage of the cool of night to move.

It is imperative that all hives be perfectly tight at the joints and well nailed so that there may be no leakage of bees. Even then it is no uncommon occurrence to have bees come out from some partly concealed knot-hole or partially rotted bottom-board. A package of coarse absorbent cotton will answer well for such an emergency. It will not only quickly stop the leak but has the effect of repelling the bees. Wet clay may be used in an emergency.

For moving, the hives should be closed when all field bees are at home so as to have no loss. This can be done in the evening or early morning.

Entrances should be screened but not totally blocked as the bees need air exchange during transport. If possible strap the hives or at least use hive staples to keep the hive parts from shifting and coming apart.

Fig. 39. Hives screened for moving in hot weather.

Use care in hauling not to jar or jerk the hives any more than can be possibly helped. Avoid all excitement or heat to the bees, especially at the start of the haul. For overland hauling, hives should be loaded with the frames running crosswise of the wagon or truck, on railroad cars, lengthwise.

If it is necessary to haul with wagons and horses, too much caution against having trouble with escaping bees and consequent stinging cannot be taken. Immediately any trouble is encountered, teams should be unhooked and gotten away from the angry bees until all is quiet.

Moving Short Distances

It may be necessary to change location of the out-yard only a small distance, say a few hundred yards. This can be done very nicely in the evening or early morning, taking care to handle all as carefully as possible, and it may not be necessary even to close the entrances.

It should be borne in mind, however, that many bees, unless precautions are taken, may take flight without noticing the change in location, and on returning, go back to the old location and be lost. To avoid this, the shade board or other suitable board may be leaned in front of the entrance that outgoing bees may notice the change of location at once and mark it, similarly to the manner in which young bees mark their home when making their first flights from the hive.

Even with these precautions some bees may return to the old location. These may be saved by leaving one or two weak colonies for a few days at the old location to catch the drifting bees as their return.

Moving a Few Miles

If the weather be cool and the bees can be transported to the new location in a very short time, it may not be necessary to provide special ventilation during the haul. The hives may be closed, entrances and all. But it is better to err on the side of too much ventilation than too little. The hauling at evening or in the early morning, to take advantage of lower temperature, will help.

Very often beekeepers, in such moving, provide clustering room by placing an empty super above each brood chamber, into which the bees can cluster, thus relieving the congestion on the combs below. Some combine this with a screened entrance while still others would not attempt to move even a short distance without a part of the top of the hive screened. A screened entrance is objectionable as the old bees, accustomed to fly out through it, worry themselves to death before it.

Fig. 40. Moving an apiary 75 miles by auto truck.

When releasing the bees at the end of the haul, it may be wise to allow them to become quiet before opening. At any rate it will be well to have the smoker handy to prevent an excited rush from the entrance with consequent confusion, drifting of bees, etc.

Fig. 41. How one California queen-breeder moves their outfit to a new- location.

The Long Haul

Probably a large proportion of the moving trips of the out-apiarist will be over a distance of from ten to fifty miles, either in the establishment of a new yard or in moving an apiary to new pastures by the migratory plan already mentioned. The colonies may have to be moved when heavy with honey or brood, or when the weather is very hot.

In such instances it is well-nigh indispensable to provide clustering room and ventilation for the trip by having the whole of the top of the hive screened, the moving screen being two or more inches deep, with proper reinforcements over the top to prevent breakage. In rare instances the bottom-boards may be removed and the bottoms of the hives screened also.

Fig. 42. The truck is fast replacing the slower wagon, for moving bees.

Fig. 43. Where the haul is short and the weather cool, colonies may be moved with the covers on.

It may be necessary to give the bees water during the haul, should they become excited. Water is needed only when they have young brood.

The up-to-date migratory beekeeper provides themselves with moving screens, tight hives, and suitable hauling conveyances to take best care of the number of colonies they propose to move. Edson Brothers of California, as an example, operate 2500 colonies of bees practically all of which are moved to the orange and the bean fields for these flows. They have a four ton truck with a capacity of a whole yard of 100 colonies, moving screens and all. Thus they care for a unit of one apiary at a trip. Their moving is done in the night.

Today's migratory beekeepers haul bees across the USA on semi tractor-trailer setups. These bees are placed on four way pallets, loaded on the trailer and large nets are placed over the entire load to contain any stray bees. Semi loads usually consist of 480 colonies per load.

Rail Shipments

As in the long overland haul, ample ventilation should be provided. The trip is apt to be prolonged by delays. Hives should be loaded with frames running in the same direction as the rails as much of the jarring comes from starting and stopping of trains and switching.

Fig. 44. "Old Sally," a seemingly indestructible car in the Dadant outapiary system, seeing service in moving bees a short distance.

Colonies should usually be loaded so that it may be possible to inspect any colony at any time, and one or two barrels of water should be provided in case of necessity.

A thing most often neglected in shipping cars of bees is the bracing of the hives sufficiently to prevent jamming, with consequent loosening of joints, leakage of bees and excitement.

Probably only a small proportion of outapiarists will have more than a rare experience in moving bees by this method, yet there are locations where it may be advisable to move long distances to reach new and heavy flows. This is done by some of California's best beekeepers who go to the alfalfa regions of Nevada and Utah each year.

M.G. Dadant

CHAPTER XII

AUTOMOBILES AND TRUCKS

The automobile has done more than any other one thing to revolutionize outapiary beekeeping. Its adaptability to extensive beekeeping is self-evident. It furnishes a quick mode of travel from one apiary to another, it travels in the heat as well as in cooler weather, it removes the danger of stings to horses when used in the apiary. The Dadants succeed in moving 500 colonies, with trucks, nowadays, more readily than the elder Dadant succeeded in moving 100 colonies in 1880 on hay-racks.

Fig. 45. A light pleasure car with commodious box on the rear is a prime requisite in the small outapiary system. Miss Mathilda Candler of Wisconsin.

Then, too, motive power is necessary during only a fraction of the year for outapiary work. The car may be put away for the balance of the year with a minimum amount of upkeep. It is often necessary to remain at the out-yard till late in the evening to replace wet supers, etc. The use of the automobile shortens the hours of the apiarist.

Modern beekeeping may call for many moves of colonies or equipment. These are transported with the least jar and in the least time by the auto truck.

Type of Car to Use

Pleasure cars are most generally used by the beekeepers, either in their original form or improved by the addition of a box or bed at the back to facilitate the hauling of supers, extracting equipment and other apiary supplies. Not a few are later converted into light trucks to suit the expanding needs of the apiarist.

The light pleasure car has the advantage of being faster, of costing less for running and for upkeep. Yet it has its limits. Other provisions would have to be made by the beekeeper for hauling honey home from extracting houses, for hauling bees and other heavy equipment.

The question resolves itself into just what style of car is cheapest and yet will adapt itself most readily to the system of each individual beekeeper. Depreciation, upkeep, interest on the investment, mileage costs, and time on the road are all to be considered.

For instance, a heavy two or three ton truck would be unexcelled for hauling large loads of honey, but the depreciation of a $2500.00 machine carried over a period of ten years would amount to at least $250.00 per year and interest on the investment would add another $150.00 making a yearly cost of $400.00 not to mention running and upkeep costs which would be much greater on the larger machine.

Fig. 46. A big three ton truck hauling ready cased honey in
California.

Would it not be more economical to use the smaller truck
to reduce costs, or even a light delivery car and have the
heavy hauling done by hired machines? Evidently it would
be unless the apiary system were large enough to warrant
the extra expense.

The light car or converted machine would be most
economical with a system of four or less apiaries. For five
or more, the light truck with a capacity of one ton might be
best, while with the larger systems a heavy truck would in
all likelihood prove worth its extra cost. But the large truck,
if hauling bees to any extent, would be improved with
pneumatic tires throughout.

Fig. 47. Trailer pulled by a pleasure car, bringing in a load of comb honey in cases

Fig. 48. Another type of trailer often encountered.

With the large truck also, a small delivery car for ordinary trips would be a necessity. In the central plant system, a truck of some description is a necessity, as it is in migratory beekeeping practiced regularly. Morley Pettit, of Ontario, furnishes an example of the former, using a one-ton Ford truck. Edson Brothers of California are instances of the latter, having a four ton truck for their 2,500 colonies. With this number, the larger truck should pay.

The tendency seems to be towards a truck of a capacity of from one to two tons, as the Ford, Dodge, light Republic, or similar car.

Trailers

Not a few beekeepers provide themselves with trailers to be attached to the regular highly geared car, for emergency in super hauling, moving of bees, etc. For the occasional light haul this will do, but it is hardly satisfactory for much heavy hauling or daily work. The chances of trouble from overloading and breaking down are too great.

Launches

Where streams are available the launch furnishes the ideal method of transportation, though it is slower than the automobile in good weather and on good roads.

Launches are especially desirable, since there is practically no jar while moving and losses are brought to a minimum.

Fig. 49. For transporting bees, there is nothing better than the launch.

This method of handling out-yards is popular in the swampy regions of Florida. It is there almost the only means available and bees are placed on scaffolds raised above high water mark.

Motorcycles

Not a few beekeepers, of the East especially, have found it advantageous to use motorcycles, having all other hauling done by hired vehicles. This is to be recommended where the apiarist lives in the city and has another occupation during the winter months, with no use for automobile or truck during eight months of the year.

L. F. Howden of New York estimated that their motorcycle will carry him 100 miles on 1/2 gallon of gasoline. It will carry fifty pounds of equipment with ease, and this is all that is necessary for most of the trips. The investment is small, and upkeep insignificant, compared with the larger machine or truck.

CHAPTER XIII

HONEY-HOUSES AND EQUIPMENT

In no part of the equipment of the outapiarist is there such a wide range of difference as in the style of honey-house used. This is due, not only to the system practiced by the beekeeper, but also to their financial condition, and to the buildings which might have been available when each apiary was established.

Yet we may say that the requirements for a honey-house, in almost all instances, are the same with the same system, the difference in houses coming from the fact that many apiarists do without certain conveniences or requirements for one reason or another.

Requirements

The ideal honey-house should be large enough to care for all operations and extra equipment of the apiary at its maximum. Nine-tenths of the houses built are outgrown in the course of a few years, with the result that the apiarist hesitates to rebuild and does with the little room to the detriment of their work.

The usual mistake is to make the side-walls of the house too shallow. Extracting supers can be piled to a height of fifteen shallow supers as well as ten, so the distance to the eaves may be nine feet as well as six or seven.

If the house is but one story high, with a gable roof, considerable storage space for little used articles should be provided under the gables and above ordinary reaching height. Light articles such as extra frames, empty supers, etc., may be well stored there. Coggshall of New York, writing many years ago, advised making the out-yard house double the capacity figured as sufficient for the beekeeper's needs.

Another mistake too often made is in not making the house strong enough to stand the jar of the extractor or the weight of such honey as may be stored within the building.

Concrete floors are desirable, but should be placed high enough, when building, so that they will be above the surrounding ground, else the drainage will be towards the house rather than away from it.

The house should be bee-tight and mouse proof. There is nothing more annoying nor more apt to make angry bees and trouble than a leaky house during a honey dearth or at extracting time. The ordinary carpenter does not realize the value of such a point to the beekeeper and will almost invariably neglect to make all tight around the eaves, along the joists of the floor, or the lumber they use may shrink enough to leave cracks for bees.

A very good way to avoid trouble is to cover the framework of the house entirely with tarred paper before putting on the siding, floor, or roof. Tar is obnoxious to bees and they will hesitate to enter where a tar smell is predominant.

Mice are an aggravation, but are easily disposed of. Certain it is that extracting supers should be mouse proof, or the loss from eaten and damaged combs may be considerable.

Windows in the modern house are a necessity. These should be made to slide sideways so as not to trap bees, and openings should be covered with screen which will allow the bees to go out at the top, while preventing their re-entrance. The usual plan is to extend the screen for two feet above the top of the window. The bees will readily run up but will seldom find their way down such a long distance. Honey-house escapes are used much in connection with window openings.

Many beekeepers think it a mistake to let bees out before the end of the day's work, since it is apt to draw more robbers around the house. They have window screens closed during the day to be readily opened at evening to let out the accumulation of bees.

Fig. 50. Bees clustering around a screened window, trying to get to the sweets inside.

It is hardly desirable to have a screened door. The bees will congregate there at each trip that we make with honey. If a screened door is desired it should be made in the form of an entry as shown in the accompanying cut. Most of the bees lose themselves between the two doors and are trapped in the entry to run out at openings in the screen at the top.

Fig. 51. Screened entry to the honey-house that will keep the bees out.

Make your honey-house door wide. If barrels are used for honey storage the house door should be large enough to pass the barrel without shunting it back and forth, or standing it on end. wheelbarrows, hand-barrows, large extractors and other equipment should pass through readily.

Location of the House

The honey-house should be located as handy to the apiary as possible. If on a slope, it should be slightly below the apiary to make for case in hauling full supers of honey down. Ordinarily it will be handiest at the side of the apiary, or at the back, rather than in the center or in front, and doors should be so located as to give best results both for hauling in from the apiary and for loading and hauling honey away.

Fig. 52. A temporary house in use in a Texas apiary system.

Types of Houses

Where a fairly good building is available it will hardly be necessary to build specially. When comb honey is raised or if extracting is done centrally, it will only be necessary to have a house large enough for storage. In fact many apiaries are handled without any honey house at all. In the migratory system this is the rule rather than the exception. Yet some sort of a shelter should be provided for extra equipment if it is to be left out for any length of time.

Temporary Houses

The temporary cloth house is used by many where the apiary is located only for a short time. Many years ago, in the France apiaries, such houses were used. These were put up at the time of extracting and were taken down and removed to the next apiary as fast as the crew extracted. In this case rough shelter was provided for extra equipment the year around. The Frances have since changed their methods because they now have permanent yards, and permanent houses were built in connection.

AV. L. Chambers, of Arizona, has been another extensive user of the temporary cheese cloth shelter for extracting. These houses may be made large to allow ample room for extracting, since their cost is small and the labor in setting up, insignificant.

Temporary extracting rooms in the form of tents are much used. They are a makeshift, being hot in summer and not bee proof.

The Portable House

Since the earliest days of out-yard beekeeping, portable outfits, mounted on heavy wagons or drays, have been used. In these, space is conserved as much as possible and only necessary equipment for extracting is carried. One description calls for a bed 4 feet wide and 12 feet long, a rather small extracting room. In such, naturally, honey storage receptacles are outside the house and supers are removed as fast as extracted, either to be replaced on the hives or piled up and covered.

The big truck has made a change in construction of these portable outfits. They are now large enough to house the modern extracting equipment and the power of the truck is sufficient to haul the most complex equipment desirable.

These portable extracting outfits mounted on auto-trucks are very popular in the West and more especially in California where migratory beekeeping is practiced, and where the same location may not be desired two years in succession.

Sectional Houses

Several Michigan beekeepers and others use sectional houses for apiaries which are fairly permanent, where it may be necessary to move location a short distance from time to time. These are well built houses of lumber with each side, roof and floor, in sections, to be easily taken down. They are made large enough for the needs of the apiary the year round, and when well put up can be made bee-tight. Easily taken down, they can be loaded on a wagon or truck and rapidly transported to a new location

Fig. 54. Honey-house built so that it may be readily cut apart into sections and removed. Where the cut is to be made, rafters or studding are placed within an inch of each other and holes bored so that the sections may be drawn together with bolts when set up again.

The Permanent House

By far the larger percentage of apiary houses are of permanent construction, carefully built, oftentimes with cement floor and large enough to house all extra equipment. The most of them are used in connection with a portable extracting outfit, though not a few are equipped with a permanent one.

Fig. 55. Honey-house built with ample ventilation for extracting.

A house of such construction, designed for an apiary of 100 colonies, should be made at least 16 feet wide and 20 feet long, while a larger house would be a convenience; the size desirable, of course, being dependent upon the complexity of extracting outfit, on the system of supering, and also upon whether honey is to be hauled home as fast as extracted, or stored at the out-yard until sold. Many have storage tanks in connection, running the honey by gravity directly into the honey tank.

Not a few such houses are made two or more stories high, to allow of honey packing, carpenter work, etc., with well-built cellar for wintering beneath. These involve extra investment but are exceedingly desirable when conditions warrant them.

Fig. 56. A France outapiary house with cellar beneath which serves as winter cellar.

Fig. 57. Central extracting plant of K. E. Sutton in Colorado. All honey is hauled in from outapiaries, to be extracted.

The Central Plant

The central extracting plant has many features which make it attractive to the outapiarist so located as to make such a system practicable. Having all equipment in one building and all expenditures for houses to be embodied in one central house, it is possible to so plan as to include, in this one, all modern equipment advantageous for running several hundred colonies of bees.

This plan is much favored by any beekeeper who has once practiced it, and we have to hear of a single instance where the central plant was given up when once tried. Almost all beekeepers using this plan, however, have had previous experience with out-yard work and were able to judge whether it would fit in with their system of management before they made the change.

Fig. 58. Central plant of the Jager apiaries in Minnesota. This is one of the most complete buildings of its kind anywhere.

The central plant must be a roomy, well ventilated and a well lighted building, with arrangements for power for the extractors, elevators, saws, pump, etc. A steam plant may be installed for heating honey, rendering wax, for the knife and capping melter as well as for heating the building, and it should be equipped with a water system and in fact almost any equipment which makes for cleanliness and labor saving. Its interior should be so divided as to provide a separate room for each operation.

For the reader's information we can do no better than to quote a description of the central plant of the Pettit apiaries as described by Mr. Morley Pettit in the American Bee Journal.

"The building is 24 x 40 feet with walls 16 feet to the plate, and a gable roof. It is built on a concrete foundation and is two stories high with a 4 inch cement floor downstairs and a pine floor on 10 inch joists overhead. The joists are 12 feet long and meet on a middle partition, making a floor strong enough to carry almost any weight that is likely to be put on it."

"The ground floor is divided by the middle partition which stops 11 feet from one end for the garage, running across the building and extending six feet in front. This garage being about 11 X 30 feet has room for a truck and an automobile or two light trucks, as required. The other two rooms, each 12 x 29 feet are the extracting room and honey-room respectively. It is ten feet from the lower to the upper floor, giving a ceiling 9 feet in the clear. The cement foundation of walls rises four inches above the cement floor which slopes towards the middle of each room, where a bell-trap connects with the sewer. This makes washing down the floor with hose and brush, after each day's extracting or other mussy work, a pleasure to anticipate. The extracting room also has a washing sink with draining table against the middle partition near the door of the honey room. Running water, hot and cold, and steam will be on tap at the sink."

"The upstairs contains the office of the business, a lavatory with closet, and shower for the men, the carpenter shop, paint shop, foundation room, store room, etc. As far as possible I aim to have a room devoted to each line of work and use it for nothing else. Then machinery and appliances once installed need not be moved, but can be left all ready for use at a moment's notice. It is a lot of space, but that is cheaper than man-time, which is about the most expensive commodity there is in production today."

Interior Arrangements

It would be impossible to give sufficient details of different interior arrangements of honey-houses without creating confusion in the minds of the reader. Naturally the arrangement will be worked out by each beekeeper as that best suited to their needs. There are, however, details of interior arrangement which, if mentioned, may be of benefit in planning.

An ideal way is to have the honey, as it comes to the house, loaded onto a tram car or else a car with overhead track which leads directly to the uncapping-can or box which should, above all, be placed in the best lighted spot in the room. Next to the uncapping box should be a dripping box for uncapped combs, and next to this the extractor, all being in such close proximity that the combs may be handled from the uncapper to the man at the extractor without unnecessary steps.

Fig, .59. Interior arrangement of one of AI. H. Mendleson's honey-houses in California.

Fig, 60. A. A. Lyons of Colorado runs two power extractors in their central plant. One is going while the other is being loaded.

Very often the honey comes in on a cool day and may become so stiff as to be difficult in uncapping and extracting. A well heated room where these combs from the apiary may be stored and heated for a short time before going to the extracting room, will be of advantage.

There is a decided advantage in having storage room below the regular extracting room also. In this manner, extractor and uncapping box may be directly connected with storage tanks by down-pipes. Herman Rauchfuss, in Colorado, uses this method and has the pipes leading from the extractor and uncapping box steam jacketed so that the honey on its way down is heated. It is drawn from the settling tanks into containers before becoming cold, so that it is very slow to granulate.

Many houses have cement bases for extractors and some are made on two levels so that the extractor may be placed directly on the floor and the honey drawn off a step or two below. Some run two extractors in combination so that one may be loading while the other is extracting, making for time saving.

Very often it may be advisable to have stove or steam generating plant for the honey knife or cappings melter outside the building to avoid heat. It is wise to have a large boiler for generating steam for the knife that it may always be hot. Very often, with a small boiler and cold honey, steam will not be generated as fast as needed.

Power for the extractor is generally furnished by a gasoline engine. The engine should be bought sufficiently large so that it will carry an extra load of a second extractor or of other equipment should such be needed later.

Fig. 61. Settling tanks and heating system are in the basement of the Sutton central plant.

Where electric power is available a motor instead of a gas engine is desirable. The motor is cleaner, easier running and more economical. It can be turned on when ready and stopped during intervals when desired.

I would urge upon all beekeepers, keeping a cost account of the different operations in outapiary honey production. Especially is this desirable with the use of trucks. In no other way can the beekeeper be sure that they are using the most economical system in caring for their bees. So far, beekeeping has been carried on by the hit or miss system and without any idea of costs such as have helped build up the large businesses of today.

ABOUT THE AUTHOR

Wayne Flewelling, JR is the owner and operator of John and Wayne Honey Farm LLC located at Quenemo, KS. He has been keeping bees since 2003 and had been locally recognized for his dedication to his bees and beekeeping. He has appeared on Ag AM in Kansas and has written articles for local and national publications. He recently has expanded his operation to include queen and NUC production as well.

M.G. Dadant

M.G. Dadant

www.ingramcontent.com/pod-product-compliance
Lightning Source LLC
Chambersburg PA
CBHW071201280526
45787CB00002B/561